BTPL

KU-134-711

501 237 925

SCIENCE ANSWERS

Food Chains and Webs

FROM PRODUCERS TO DECOMPOSERS

Richard and Louise Spilsbury

Heinemann
LIBRARY

501237925

www.heinemann.co.uk/library
Visit our website to find out more information about **Heinemann Library** books.

To order:
 Phone 44 (0) 1865 888066
 Send a fax to 44 (0) 1865 314091
Visit the Heinemann Bookshop at www.heinemann.co.uk/library to browse our catalogue and order online.

First published in Great Britain by Heinemann Library, Halley Court, Jordan Hill, Oxford OX2 8EJ, part of Harcourt Education.

Heinemann is a registered trademark of Harcourt Education Ltd.

© Harcourt Education Ltd 2004
The moral right of the proprietor has been asserted.

All rights reserved. No part of this publication may be reproduced, stored in a retrieval system, or transmitted in any form or by any means, electronic, mechanical, photocopying, recording, or otherwise, without either the prior written permission of the publishers or a licence permitting restricted copying in the United Kingdom issued by the Copyright Licensing Agency Ltd, 90 Tottenham Court Road, London W1T 4LP (www.cla.co.uk).

Editorial: Nancy Dickmann and Tanvi Rai
Design: Richard Parker and Celia Floyd
Illustrations: John Fleck
Picture Research: Rebecca Sodergren and Pete Morris
Production: Séverine Ribierre

Originated by Dot Gradations Ltd
Printed in China by WKT Company Limited

ISBN 0 431 17513 6
08 07 06 05 04
10 9 8 7 6 5 4 3 2 1

British Library Cataloguing in Publication Data
Spilsbury, Richard and Louise
Food Chains and Webs. – (Science Answers)
577.1'6
A full catalogue record for this book is available from the British Library.

Acknowledgements
The publishers would like to thank the following for permission to reproduce photographs: Corbis/Bettmann **p. 28**; FLPA/Fritz Polking **p. 7**; FLPA/Minden Pictures **pp. 8, 9**; FLPA/Steve Maslowski **p. 26**; FLPA/Wendy Dennis **p. 18**; Getty Images/Digital Vision **p. 6**; Getty/photodisc **p. 29**; Harcourt Education Ltd/Tudor Photography **pp. 23, 27**; NHPA/B. & C. Alexander **p. 22**; NHPA/Bill Coster **p. 15**; NHPA/Daniel Heuclin **p. 17**; NHPA/Guy Edwards **p. 5**; NHPA/Hellio & Van Ingen **p. 19**; NHPA/Image Quest 3D **p. 11**; NHPA/Jany Sauvanet **p. 23**; NHPA/Norbert WU **p. 13**; NHPA/Stephen Dalton **pp. 21, 25**; Oxford Scientific Films **pp. 12, 14**.

Cover photograph of an osprey catching a fish reproduced with permission of FLPA/Fritz Polking.

Every effort has been made to contact copyright holders of any material reproduced in this book. Any omissions will be rectified in subsequent printings if notice is given to the publishers.

The paper used to print this book comes from sustainable resources.

Contents

What are food chains and webs? 4

What types of food webs are found in grasslands? 8

Who eats whom in oceans, rivers and lakes? 11

What are the food webs in dry places? 17

Who eats whom in forests? 21

What are the food webs in towns and cities? 25

People who found the answers 28

Amazing facts 29

Glossary 30

Index 32

More books to read 32

Any words appearing in bold, **like this**, are explained in the Glossary.

About the experiments and demonstrations

This book contains some boxes headed 'Science Answers'. Each one describes an experiment or demonstration that you can try yourself. In doing them you will get a chance to research and make your own food chains and webs, to show the feeding relationships in a variety of habitats.

Materials you will use

Most of the experiments and demonstrations in this book can be done with objects that you can find in your own home. You will also need a pencil and paper to record your results.

What are food chains and webs?

A food chain or web is a diagram that shows a series of living things that eat each other to get **energy**. Plants and animals need energy to live. The Sun is the source of all energy on Earth. Plants trap this energy to make their own food. Animals get energy by eating plants or other animals that eat plants.

How do food chains work?

Every living thing is like a link in a food chain. The first link in a chain could be a leaf. Then a slug eats the leaf. A toad eats the slug. In this way, energy is passed from one link to the next.

What are food webs like?

Most animals eat more than one kind of food. This means that they are part of two or more food chains. The different food chains connect with each other to form food webs.

How are food chains and webs different?

A food chain follows a simple line, like a chain (see berries/vole/lynx). Food chains joined together form a more complicated web, which looks rather like a spider's web when you draw it. Note that in a food web, an arrow is drawn from each **organism** pointing to the organism who eats it.

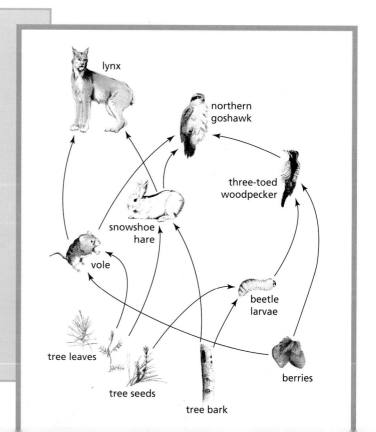

lynx

northern goshawk

three-toed woodpecker

snowshoe hare

vole

beetle larvae

tree leaves

tree seeds

tree bark

berries

4

How do food chains and webs start?

All food chains and webs start with plants. Plants trap the Sun's energy in their leaves. They use this energy to combine water and carbon dioxide (a gas from the air) to make food in the form of sugars. This process is called **photosynthesis**. Plants are known as **producers** because they produce (make) food.

How do leaves trap energy?

Plant leaves trap the energy in sunlight to make food. They use a substance called chlorophyll to do this, and it is this chlorophyll that gives the leaves their green colour.

Animals are **consumers**. They consume (eat) plants to get the energy stored inside them, or they eat other animals, which have eaten the plants. **Herbivores** are animals that feed mainly on plant parts, such as leaves, seeds, berries or nuts. **Carnivores** are animals that eat other animals. **Omnivores** are animals that eat both plants and animals. When these animals die, **scavengers** and **decomposers** eat their remains and break them down to get energy.

What are primary and secondary consumers?

Plants produce food for themselves, but animals take advantage of this food supply by eating it themselves. Herbivores are called primary consumers because they are the first to eat plant food and therefore the first to consume some of this energy. Secondary consumers are animals that eat primary consumers. Carnivores, scavengers and decomposers are all secondary consumers. Omnivores are both primary and secondary consumers because they eat both plants and other plant-eating animals!

Decomposers and energy recycling

When a plant or animal dies, the energy in its body is not wasted. Decomposers, such as **fungi** and **bacteria**, feed on the remains of living things. Decomposers break them down into tiny pieces, some of which they use and some of which get washed into the soil. Plants take in some of this goodness from the soil when they take in water through their roots, and they use it to grow.

Fruit fans

This orang-utan is a primary consumer. It is a herbivore that lives off mainly plant parts that it finds in the forests of South-East Asia. Its favourite meal is fruit!

How many links do food chains have?

The number of links in a single food chain is usually only four or five. Each living thing in the chain uses up some energy to do things such as grow and move, so energy is continually being lost as it is passed along the food chain. This is why food webs always have more producers than primary consumers, and more primary consumers than secondary consumers. For example, in African grassland **savannah** there are more grass plants than there are zebras that eat them, and more zebras than there are lions that eat them!

Habitats and food chains

A place where an animal or plant lives is called its **habitat**. Different habitats contain different **organisms** that are **adapted** (suited) to life within them. In this book we will look at different kinds of habitats and a sample of the food chains and webs within them.

What types of food webs are found in grasslands?

Grasslands are places where the soil is too poor or the weather too dry for trees and many other plants to grow. Instead, tough wild grasses take over the land. These form the basis of grassland food chains.

Tropical grasslands are called **savannahs**. Tropical places have a dry and a rainy season, and savannahs have scattered trees and shrubs. Some grasslands grow in areas with hot summers and cold winters and have few trees. These are called **prairies** in America, pampas in Argentina and steppes in Asia.

Primary consumers

Small and large **herbivores graze** on the different kinds of grasses in the world's grasslands. Many butterflies, bees and other insects feed on **nectar** from grass plant flowers, and caterpillars, beetles and grasshoppers munch the leaves.

Ants and anteaters

South American giant anteaters, like this one, are about the size of Alsatian dogs. They eat up to 30,000 grassland ants and termites a day, catching them with their long sticky tongues. The insects are primary consumers that feed on grassland plants.

Many grassland herbivores are **rodents**, with sharp front teeth for gnawing. They eat grass seeds and roots, as well as leaves. Grassland rodents include the cavy in the pampas, marmots and lemmings in the steppes, and deer mice, voles and prairie dogs in the prairies. Many of these rodents also feed on grassland insects and spiders, which makes them **secondary** as well as **primary consumers**.

What are prarie dogs?

Prairie dogs are not dogs at all. They are rodents that feed on prairie grasses and sometimes insects. They live in underground homes called burrows.

Large grassland herbivores

There are also many large animals that feed on grasses. Some of these are birds. Ostriches in Africa, rheas in South America and emus in Australia are all large, flightless birds that feed on grassland plants. In the African savannah there are large herds of antelopes, wildebeest and zebra. In Australia, kangaroos leap across grasslands in search of good grazing grounds. Bison and pronghorn deer graze on some parts of the American prairies.

Grassland secondary consumers

Many different kinds of animals feed on the grassland herbivores. Insects such as termites are eaten by anteaters and aardvarks in the nest, but also by lizards and snakes when they leave the nest to feed. Snakes slither underground to eat burrowing herbivores, such as the prairie dogs. Falcons, owls and hawks fly above grasslands, hunting rodents.

Some grassland **carnivores** such as lions, hyenas and hunting dogs hunt in teams. They work together to bring down big herbivores such as wildebeest. After they have eaten, vultures, who are **scavengers**, circle the air searching for the remains of the dead animal to feast on.

A prairie food web

This is a food web from a prairie **habitat**. How many individual food chains can you find within it?

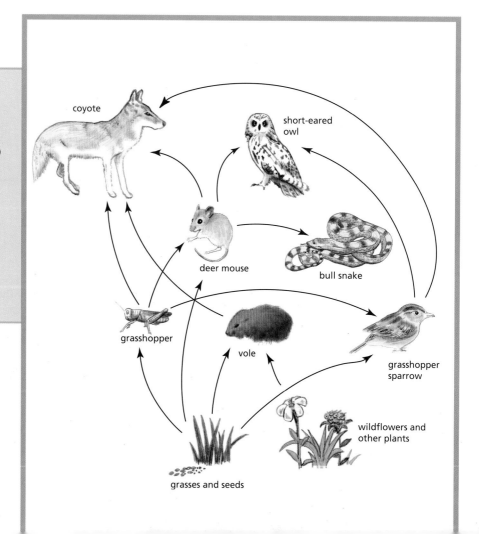

coyote

short-eared owl

deer mouse

bull snake

grasshopper

vole

grasshopper sparrow

wildflowers and other plants

grasses and seeds

Who eats whom in oceans, rivers and lakes?

The oceans of the world cover more than three-quarters of the Earth's surface and are full of life. However, few plants live in open oceans, because plants need sunlight for **photosynthesis** and the deeper the water, the less light there is. So, what are the **producers** in an ocean food web?

Ocean producers

The surface waters of the ocean look clear and empty, but they are actually packed with **plankton**. Plankton is the name given to the collection of **microscopic organisms** floating in the oceans. It is made up of plants (mostly **algae**) and tiny animals (such as fish **larvae**). The algae in plankton are the producers in any ocean food web. The billions of producers in plankton like this carry out 40 per cent of all the photosynthesis that happens on Earth!

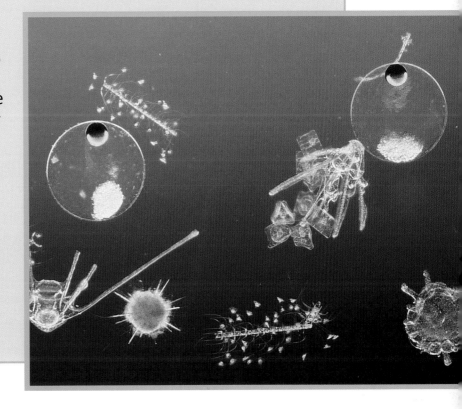

Primary consumers

The smallest ocean **consumers** live in plankton, and include tiny shrimp-like animals called copepods. Plankton also includes the larvae of animals such as crabs and jellyfish. These consumers are **herbivores**, and feed on the microscopic plants in plankton.

Secondary consumers

Larger **carnivores** such as prawn-sized **krill** eat these tiny organisms and, in turn, even larger animals such as fish and squid eat them. Seabirds, large fish such as tuna, and **mammals** such as sea lions and dolphins eat squid and other fish. The top **predators** in the world's oceans are great white sharks and orcas.

Filter-feeding giant

Remarkably, the largest animal on Earth, the blue whale, eats some of the smallest – krill. Blue whales have rows of special fringed teeth called baleen. They push mouthfuls of water through their baleen using a car-sized tongue, to trap the krill. One whale can eat up to 4 tonnes of krill each day!

Coastal food chains

Coastal waters are shallower than the open ocean. The land is covered and then exposed by rising and falling **tides** and crashing waves. Large algae called seaweeds grow attached to rocks in different depths of coastal water. Photosynthesis happens in their fronds (leaves).

Bristling barnacles

Barnacles live attached to coastal rocks. When the tide is in, they open their shells and wave their bristled legs to catch bits of food.

Some animals **graze** on algae. Molluscs are soft-bodied animals with hard, protective shells. Some, such as limpets and topshells, move over algae-covered rocks and seaweed, scraping off bits to eat using their rough tongues. Other molluscs, such as dogwhelks, drill into these grazers' shells to eat them. Cockles have two shells and live in sand. They come to the surface to feed on plankton and bits of dead organisms. Sea birds such as oystercatchers feed on the molluscs.

Rivers and lakes

Rivers and most lakes contain fresh water, not salt water like oceans. The producers in deep lakes are tiny floating algae, just like in salty oceans. In rivers and at lake edges there are larger water plants. In fast-moving water, plants such as eelgrass have long, thin leaves that do not drag and get damaged. In calmer shallow waters, plants such as water lilies are rooted at the bottom and have large leaves that float up to catch sunlight.

Freshwater feeders

The small grazers in rivers and lakes include tiny floating organisms called **protists**, and snails and tadpoles. Some insects, like water fleas, float on the water among the algae they feed on. Others, such as pond skaters, 'walk' across the surface using water surface tension, catching prey such as dead insects.

Feeding in water

Large freshwater herbivores include moose, which paddle into rivers to feed on water weed. Manatees (female and calf seen here) are large and unusual animals that hold their breath and swim slowly underwater to munch riverbed plants, often holding them with their front flippers as they eat.

Changing diet

Tadpoles graze on algae after they hatch from eggs. As adults, they turn into carnivores, hunting swimming animals in water at first and eventually insects and slugs on land.

Walking on water?

Jacana birds have very, very long toes that enable them to walk on waterlily leaves – so it looks as if they can walk on water! Jacanas are **omnivores**. They walk across floating water plants to find insects and other small animals, and plant seeds, to eat.

Freshwater secondary consumers

Some fish, such as trout, feed on insect larvae and drowned flies. Others, such as bream, feed on worms and snails from the riverbed. Predators such as pike hunt these fish. Birds such as herons strut along lake shores looking for fish to spear with their beaks.

In some African and Asian rivers, crocodiles hunt underwater **prey**, including fish and turtles. They also sometimes seize mammals such as deer that visit rivers to drink.

15

DEMONSTRATION: Drawing ocean food chains

Ocean food chains show how **energy** flows from the Sun into tiny plants then into herbivores and then into carnivores.

EQUIPMENT:
Large sheet of paper, pictures of orca, sea lion, fish, krill, diatom (drawn from a book, magazine or web page).

DEMONSTRATION STEPS:
1 Draw a horizontal line to show the ocean surface.
2 Draw the ocean organisms below the surface.
3 Now draw arrows from each organism pointing to the organism that eats it. Use information from pages 11–13 to help you.

EXPLANATION:
This is one ocean food chain, but there are many more. Any food chain shows the direction of energy flow, but not the numbers of organisms involved at each link in the chain. Do you think there would be more orcas than diatoms in an ocean, or the other way around? Are there more **primary consumers** than **secondary consumers**?

What are the food webs in dry places?

The driest areas of the world are known as deserts or tundra. The deserts of the world are extremely hot and have very little rainfall, and the land is rocky or covered in sand. Tundra are areas of land where water is frozen into ice and snow for most of the year, creating a dry and barren **habitat**.

Hot desert producers

The plants at the start of desert food chains and webs have different ways of getting the water they need to survive. Some have roots that spread far and wide to catch any available rainfall or dew that seeps into the ground. Others, such as cacti, store what water they do find in their fleshy stems. Many desert plants are **annuals** – they grow from seeds and flower for a short time only, after a burst of rain.

Jumping jerboas!

Desert plants are food for many **consumers**, including this jerboa, which jumps around on its long back legs finding seeds, roots, leaves and insects to eat.

Who eats desert plants?

Desert plants provide food and water for the **primary consumers** that feed on them. Some insects feed on the **nectar** or leaves of the flowering annuals. Many desert **herbivores** shelter underground or under rocks, out of the heat. Naked mole rats live in burrows and tunnel through the earth feeding on roots and other underground plant parts. Kangaroo rats and other **rodents** eat cactus seeds. Some desert lizards forage for fruits and leaves.

Secondary consumers in the desert

Scorpions eat spiders and some small lizards. Desert lizards eat insects, moths or smaller lizards. Like many desert animals, golden moles live in burrows to escape the heat of the Sun. They emerge to feed if they feel the movement of beetles, snakes and lizards on the surface. Some snakes, like the sidewinder, eat small rodents such as the kangaroo rat. Meerkats are **secondary consumers** and primary consumers. They feed on scorpions (as shown here) and insects, and also the roots of desert plants.

Tundra plants

Areas of tundra have short summers, but for most of the year the land is covered in snow or ice. Some tundra plants, such as moss, grow in cushion shapes that trap warmth and moisture. Some, such as the Arctic dwarf willow, grow low to the ground to stay out of the path of icy winds. Some mountain flowering plants survive as seeds underground in cold times, and grow leaves and flowers in the short summers.

Tundra herbivores

Insects feed on the leaves of tundra plants. For example, in the Antarctic tiny insects called springtails eat dead moss. In summer, butterflies and bees feed on flower nectar. Some small **mammals** feed on plants too. Lemmings live in tunnels beneath the Arctic snow and eat roots and moss. Arctic hares eat plants such as the Arctic dwarf willow. Large tundra grazers include musk oxen that roam about in search of plants to eat. Reindeer scrape snow with their hooves and antlers to find plants to eat.

Camouflage

Many tundra animals, including Arctic foxes, snowy owls (seen here) and Arctic hares, have white fur or feathers. This **camouflages** them against the snow and ice to hide them from animals they are hunting, or that are hunting them.

A tundra food web

Only a few **species** of plants and animals live in the harshest tundra habitats. That is why food chains and webs from the Arctic, like this one, are fairly short.

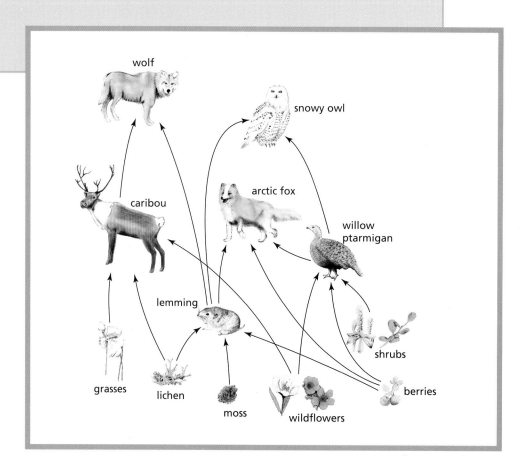

Tundra secondary consumers

Arctic foxes and birds such as snowy owls and golden eagles hunt and eat lemmings and Arctic hares. The biggest land **predators** are polar bears, which weigh up to one tonne. On tundra they eat Arctic foxes. Wolves are too small on their own to bring down large prey such as musk oxen and reindeer. They can do so when they hunt together in packs.

Who eats whom in forests?

The forests and woodlands of the world are dominated by very obvious **producers** – trees. These green plants have tall, sometimes enormous, woody stems that raise their leaves high into the air to catch sunlight for **photosynthesis**. Trees supply a wide range of **habitats** for all sorts of living things.

Many forests in temperate countries, which have warm summers and cold winters, contain deciduous trees. These drop all their delicate leaves in autumn, and survive winter on sugars stored in their trunks. The leaves that they have dropped provide food for insect **larvae**, which are eaten by birds such as tits. Many insects live and feed under tree bark and are eaten by birds such as treecreepers.

Squirrel stores

Squirrels need to bury acorns in the soil to give them a store of food for the winter. It requires a lot of **energy** to leap from tree to tree.

From primary to secondary consumer

In temperate forests, other **primary consumers** include **mammals** such as deer, beaver and porcupines that eat bark and branches. Reindeer

shelter among woodland trees and come out to **graze** on grass, young trees and shrubs. Heather is an important food for reindeer. **Secondary consumers** include **omnivores** like badgers and bears, which snuffle along the woodland floor eating anything from fruit, honey and nuts to small mammals and eggs. Woodland **carnivores** include wolves and foxes, which use their sharp teeth to trap **prey**, and **birds of prey** such as owls, which drop silently from the sky to catch small animals with their talons (claws).

A coniferous forest food chain

In temperate places, many forests contain conifers such as pine trees. The thin, waxy needle-like leaves of pines are eaten by insects such as pine sawfly larvae, which in turn are eaten by wood ants. Green woodpeckers eat wood ants. Mammals such as pine martens eat the eggs and chicks of green woodpeckers.

Tropical forests

The mighty tree producers of a tropical forest form a high canopy (top layer) that is thick with leaves, fruit and flowers. Primary consumers here include slow-moving sloths and large-nosed proboscis monkeys that eat mostly leaves. Fruit bats flap between trees in search of ripe fruit.

Secondary consumers in tropical forests include omnivores like chimps, which eat a range of food from fruit to antelopes. Carnivores include enormous spiders and centipedes that can kill birds and even mammals. Snakes climb trees to eat tree frogs, and eagles hunt monkeys. Big cats such as jaguars prowl the forest floor in search of wild pigs, deer and monkeys.

Tropical treats

The agouti is a long-legged **rodent** that eats the fruit and nuts that canopy feeders accidentally drop to the ground! Its large, sharp front teeth are strong enough to bite through tough brazil nut shells, to reach the nuts inside.

Decomposers

On the ground of all woodland and forest floors is a layer of leaf litter – fallen leaves, branches, dead plants and animals. **Bacteria** and **fungi** are the **organisms** that decompose leaf litter. As they release **nutrients** to feed themselves, they also release nutrients that are vital for trees and other plants. Fungi have networks of tiny threads under the surface that look like cotton fibres. The bits of fungi above the surface, such as mushrooms, are used for **reproduction**.

Mites, tiny worms and slugs eat fungi. Woodlice and millipedes also eat the decomposing leaf litter. Beetle larvae often eat harder rotting wood. Litter-eating **herbivores** are hunted by secondary consumers such as spiders, centipedes, shrews and salamanders.

Forest food chains

This diagram shows how food chains combine into a web in forests and woodland.

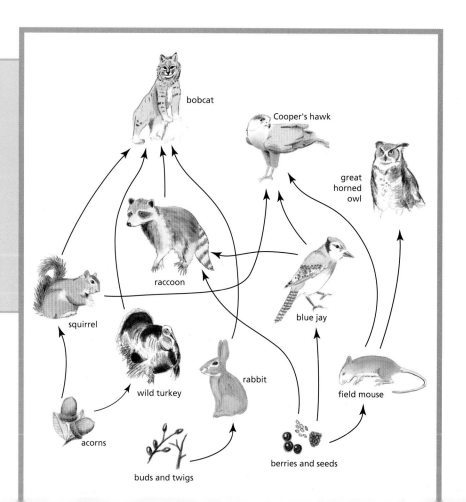

bobcat

Cooper's hawk

great horned owl

raccoon

squirrel

blue jay

wild turkey

rabbit

field mouse

acorns

berries and seeds

buds and twigs

What are the food webs in towns and cities?

Towns and cities seem unlikely places to find food chains and webs. In fact, many animals live in different **habitats** here, such as parks and gardens. Some animals eat the same food as they would in the countryside; others feed on people's waste. Note that the biggest **consumers** in towns and cities are humans.

Parks and gardens

Animals that form food chains in parks and gardens usually eat the same kinds of food as they would in the wild. The plants and trees in gardens and parks attract many butterflies, bees and other insects that feed on **nectar** and **pollen**. Worms live under lawns and birds and hedgehogs eat them. Slugs and snails **graze** on garden plants. Toads and birds eat the snails and slugs. The main **predators** here are pet cats, which eat lots of birds and small garden **mammals** such as voles.

Bird food

In autumn and winter, birds feed on the plentiful berries on bushes in parks and gardens. They also eat small animals, like this male robin which has captured a worm and brought it back to its garden-shed nest, to feed its hungry chicks.

Houses and streets

When people take over natural habitats, some of the animals that lived there are forced to move into towns and cities, where they eat very different food to what they would live on in the wild. Indoors, houseflies eat human food, and cockroaches eat all sorts of things, including food scraps and even soap! Rats and mice chew holes in cupboards and packages to get at food stored in our homes.

On the street, foxes, bears and racoons (shown here) scavenge waste food from dustbins. Gulls and pigeons eat scraps from the streets and from rubbish dumps.

Night-time flyers

Many animals living in towns and cities feed at night, when there are few people about and they cannot be seen. Barn owls swoop down from the air to feed on small animals such as voles. Bats fly around street lamps snatching insects from the air.

DEMONSTRATION: Drawing human food chains

Drawing food chains that include people can help to show that we get **energy** from our food, just like other animals, and that our food comes from plants, or animals that have eaten plants.

EQUIPMENT:

Large sheet of paper, pictures of different foods and drinks (such as milk, eggs, lasagne) and animals (such as cows and hens) and plants (such as wheat and grass). You could cut these pictures from magazines, draw them or download them from the internet. You will also need a photo of yourself!

DEMONSTRATION STEPS:

1 Choose some of the meals you like to eat and work out where they came from. For example, bread is made from a wheat plant. Burgers are made from beef from cows, which eat grass. Find or draw pictures of these things.

2 Put the photo of yourself at the top of the paper. Stick the other drawings or pictures in between, to show where the food you eat ultimately comes from.

3 Draw arrows pointing to you from each food that you eat and from the animal or plant that it came from.

EXPLANATION:

The food chains you have made show the direction of energy flow from primary producers to you. You are the last link in these food chains, because humans do not have any successful **predators**.

People who found the answers

John Muir (1838-1914)

John Muir was an influential Scottish explorer in the USA and other parts of the world. His writings were unusual at that time, in understanding that people are part of the web of nature and not the centre of it. Muir worked to protect wild places as national parks for all to enjoy. 'When we try to pick out anything by itself, we find it hitched to everything else in the Universe,' wrote John Muir.

Rachel Carson (1907-64)

Rachel Carson was a scientist and writer. She studied the effects of using chemicals to kill disease-carrying insects such as mosquitoes. In her book *Silent Spring*, she established that these chemicals affected lots of other creatures, from harmless insects to people. She also revealed that killing these insects has a major effect on food chains, as they provide food for birds and other animals. Her work was vital in creating laws to make sure that chemicals are safe before they are used in wild **habitats**.

Amazing facts

- Every tonne of paper that is recycled saves 17 trees. Up to 2000 trees are being cut down each minute in the world's tropical forests.

- More than half of the world's estimated 10 million **species** (different kinds) of plants and animals live in tropical forests.

- A dead leaf takes 6 weeks to decay completely in leaf litter.

- There are as many as 4 million **bacteria** in each kilogram of soil.

- Fastest **predators**: Mako sharks can swim and cheetahs can run at nearly 90 kph, but peregrine falcons can fly at over 300 kph.

- In a city, a pipistrelle bat can catch and eat up to 3000 insects in one night.

- The largest ocean predator is the sperm whale, which measures 17 metres in length and weighs 40 tonnes.

Glossary

adapt to change very gradually over millions of years to be better suited, or adapted, to life in a particular habitat

algae types of plants such as seaweeds that live in water and reproduce without seeds

annuals type of plants that grow from seed and reproduce in one growing season

bacteria tiny living things found in air, water and soil. Some bacteria are useful; some can cause disease.

birds of prey birds that catch and eat other animals for food

camouflage patterned or coloured to match its habitat so that it is not easily seen

carnivore animal that eats meat

consumer living thing that eats other living things

decomposer living thing that breaks down dead organisms, releasing nutrients

diatom marine producer with two hard, sculpted shells that form a box around its body

energy the power that all living things need in order to live, grow and do everything that they do

fungi group of living things that includes mushrooms and toadstools

graze feed mostly on grass or other low-growing plants

krill tiny, shrimp-like animals

habitat natural home of a group of plants or animals

herbivore animal that eats plants

larva (plural **larvae**) young animal that looks very different to its parents as it develops

mammals group of animals that includes humans. All mammals feed their babies milk from their own bodies and have some hair.

microscopic so small it can only be seen through a microscope

nectar sugary substance that plants make in their flowers to attract insects, which eat it

nutrients chemicals that plants and animals need in order to live

omnivore consumer that eats both plants and animals

organism living thing

photosynthesis process by which plants make their own food using carbon dioxide, water and energy from sunlight

plankton microscopic organisms that live in the surface waters of the oceans

pollen tiny, dust-like particles that contain a plant's male sex cells

prairie type of grassland with hot summers and cold winters where few trees grow

predator animal that hunts and catches other animals

prey animal that is caught and eaten by another animal

primary consumer herbivore

producer living thing that makes food using available nutrients. Green plants are producers.

protists microscopic organisms such as amoebas

reproduction when a living thing produces young like itself

rodent type of mammal with large, gnawing teeth

savannah type of tropical grassland with dry and rainy seasons, where many trees and bushes grow

scavenger animal that eats dead organisms and other waste it finds

secondary consumer animal that eats a herbivore

species group of living things that are very similar. Males and females of the same species can breed to produce healthy offspring.

tide rise and fall of the sea caused by the movement of the Moon

Index

algae 11, 13, 14, 15
animals 4–10, 14-15, 17–22, 23, 25, 26, 29
anteaters 8, 10

bacteria 6, 24, 29
bats 26, 29
birds 9, 10, 12, 13, 15, 19–22, 25, 26, 29

camouflage 19
carnivores 5, 6, 10, 12, 15, 22, 23
Carson, Rachel 28
chlorophyll 5
consumers 5–10, 12, 16, 17, 18, 20, 22, 23, 25

deer 19, 20, 22
deserts 17-18

energy 4, 5, 7, 16, 21, 27

fish 11, 12, 15
food chains and webs 4-5, 7, 10, 11, 16, 17, 20, 24, 27, 28
forests and woodlands 21-3, 29
fungi 6, 24

grasslands 7, 8-10
grazers 8, 13, 14, 19, 25

habitats 7, 17, 21, 25, 28
herbivores 5, 6, 8, 9, 12, 14, 18, 19, 22, 23, 24
humans 25, 27

insects 8, 10, 14, 18, 19, 21, 22, 25, 28, 29

jerboas 17

mammals 12, 19, 22, 25
manatees 14
meerkats 18
molluscs 13
Muir, John 28

oceans, rivers and lakes 11-16, 29
omnivores 5, 6, 15, 22, 23

parks and gardens 25
photosynthesis 5, 11, 13, 21
plankton 11, 12
plants 4–11, 14, 17, 18, 19, 21, 25, 29
prairie dogs 9
predators and prey 12, 15, 20, 22, 25, 27, 29
primary and secondary consumers 6, 7, 8, 9, 10, 12, 16, 18, 20, 22, 23
producers 5, 6, 7, 11, 21
protists 14

rodents 9, 18, 23, 26

savannahs 7, 8, 10
scavengers and decomposers 5, 6, 10, 24, 26
snakes 10, 18, 23
squirrels 21

towns and cities 25-6, 29
trees 21, 22, 23, 25, 29
tundra 17, 19-20

whales 12, 29

More books to read

Amazing Nature: Feasting Feeders, Tim Knight (Heinemann Library, 2003)
Amazing Nature: Powerful Predators, Tim Knight (Heinemann Library, 2003)
Living Things: Food Chains and Webs, Anita Ganeri (Heinemann Library, 2001)

Titles in the *Science Answers* series include:

Hardback   0 431 17512 8

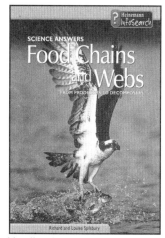

Hardback   0 431 17513 6

Hardback   0 431 17514 4

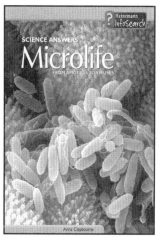

Hardback   0 431 17515 2

Hardback   0 431 17516 0

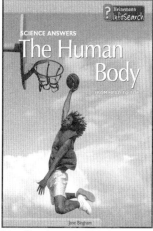

Hardback   0 431 17517 9

Find out about the other titles in this series on our website www.heinemann.co.uk/library